Stories from Faiths
Judaism

The Temple Lamp
and Other Stories

First published in the United States by
QEB Publishing, Inc.
23062 La Cadena Drive
Laguna Hills, CA 92653

www.qeb-publishing.com

Library of Congress Control Number: 2007001010

ISBN 978-1-59566-376-4

Written by Anita Ganeri
Design and editorial by East River Partnership
Illustrated by Ruth Rivers
Series Consultant Roger Butler

Publisher Steve Evans

Stories from Faiths
Judaism

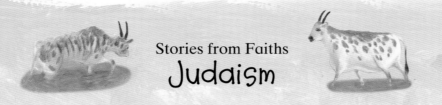

The Temple Lamp
and Other Stories

Anita Ganeri

Illustrated by Ruth Rivers

The Story of Joseph

Once, a man named Jacob had twelve sons.
His favorite son was Joseph. Jacob gave Joseph
a special present. It was a coat of many colors.

4

Joseph's brothers hated Joseph because their father loved him best. So, they threw Joseph in a deep pit and pretended that he was dead.

5

After a while, some travelers
found Joseph and took him
to Egypt. But in Egypt, a bad
person told lies about him,
and Joseph was put in prison.

In the prison, Joseph became
good at telling other prisoners
what their dreams meant.
Everything he said came true.

6

One night, the pharaoh, the ruler of Egypt, had a strange dream. He dreamed that seven fat cows came out of the river. These were followed by seven thin cows.

7

Joseph told the pharaoh what the dream meant. For the next seven years, there would be a lot of food. But, for seven years after that, there would be very little food in Egypt.

8

The pharaoh was so pleased that he let Joseph out of prison. As a reward, he gave Joseph the important job of storing spare food during the first seven years. Joseph had to make sure that the people of Egypt did not go hungry when the crops did not grow in the fields.

9

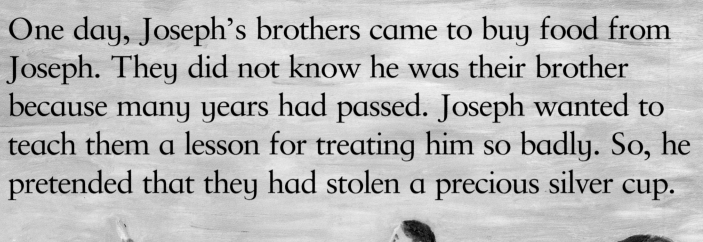

One day, Joseph's brothers came to buy food from Joseph. They did not know he was their brother because many years had passed. Joseph wanted to teach them a lesson for treating him so badly. So, he pretended that they had stolen a precious silver cup.

10

The brothers were so frightened and sorry that Joseph felt sad for them. He told them who he really was and forgave them. Soon after that, all of Joseph's family moved to Egypt to live with him.

11

The Baby in the Basket

Long ago, many Jewish people lived in Egypt. The pharaoh at that time was cruel and treated them like slaves. He made them work very hard building his palaces.

One day, the pharaoh gave an order. He told his soldiers to take every newborn Jewish baby boy and throw him into the river.

13

At that time, a Jewish woman had a baby boy. She did not want the soldiers to find him, so she hid the baby boy in her house.

14

Soon, the baby grew too
big to hide in the house.
His mother put him in
a basket and hid the
basket among the tall
reeds by the river.

15

Later that day, the pharaoh's daughter came to swim in the river. She saw the little basket and sent her maids to fetch it from the reeds.

16

When the pharaoh's daughter
looked inside the basket, she
could not believe her eyes.
There was a baby boy inside
and he was crying.

17

The pharaoh's daughter named the baby Moses.
She took Moses home to the royal palace and
brought him up as her own son.

18

Moses grew up to be an Egyptian prince, but he never forgot his Jewish family. Later, God chose Moses to be a great leader of the Jewish people.

The Story of Esther

There was once a king who ruled over a great kingdom. He lived in a splendid palace and had a beautiful wife named Esther.

20

A man named Haman helped the king rule the kingdom. Haman was always polite to the king, but very rude to other people. Nobody liked him.

21

Haman thought he was very important. He told everyone to bow when they met him. But, a Jewish man named Mordecai would not bow.

22

Haman was furious and decided to punish Mordecai and the other Jewish people. He ordered all the Jewish people in the kingdom to be killed and their things taken away.

23

The Jewish people were very frightened. Mordecai begged Queen Esther to help save them. The queen was Jewish, too, but the king did not know that.

Queen Esther thought about what to do. She dressed up in her best robes and invited the king and Haman to a special feast.

25

At the feast, brave Queen Esther told the king about Haman's wicked plan. She told the king that she was Jewish and asked him to spare her life and the lives of all the Jewish people.

The king was very angry with Haman. He ordered wicked Haman to be taken away. Then, he asked Mordecai to help him rule the kingdom, instead.

27

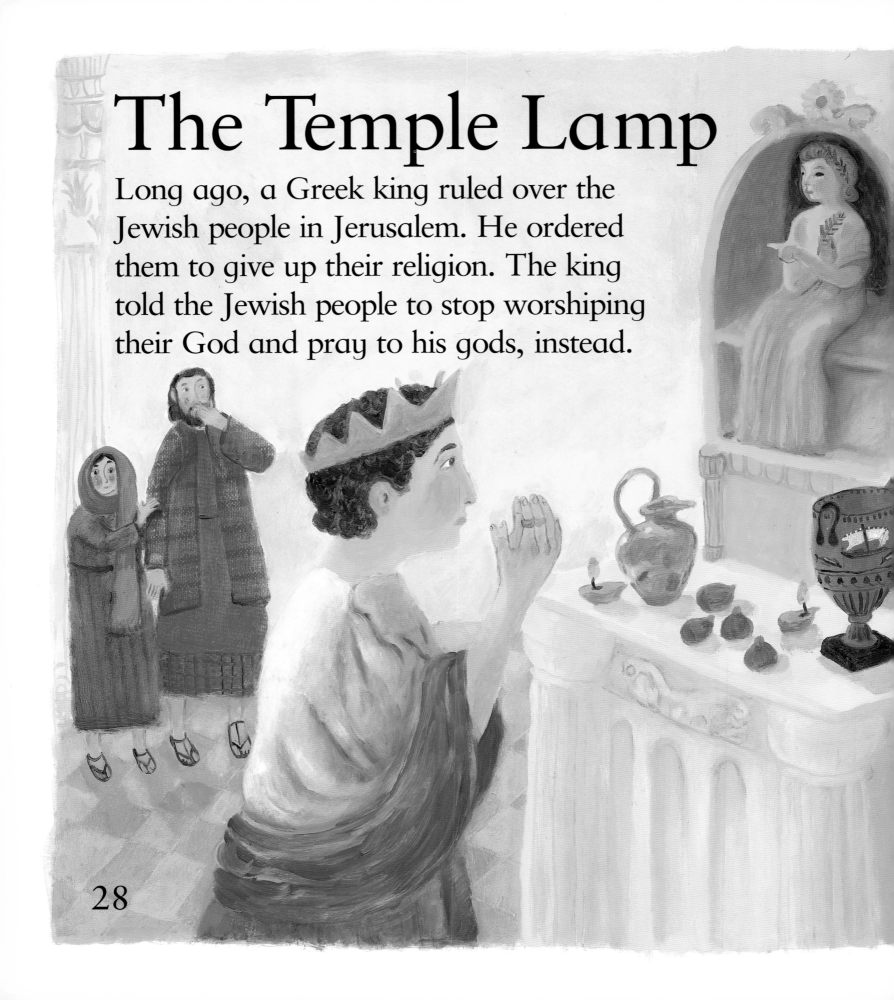

The Temple Lamp

Long ago, a Greek king ruled over the Jewish people in Jerusalem. He ordered them to give up their religion. The king told the Jewish people to stop worshiping their God and pray to his gods, instead.

28

But, the Jewish people did not obey the king. So, the king sent his soldiers to the Temple in Jerusalem. It was a very special place for Jewish people.

29

The soldiers smashed the Temple treasures. Then, they blew out the oil lamp, which always burned in the Temple. It showed that God was there.

A very brave Jewish man named Judah led an army of Jewish followers. They drove the Greek king's soldiers out of Jerusalem.

31

Judah and his followers cleaned the Temple so that the Jewish people could worship there again. Then, Judah looked for some oil to relight the Temple lamp.

But, almost every jug of oil had been broken or spilled. Then, Judah found a little jug, which had a tiny trickle of oil in the bottom.

33

But, there was only enough oil to burn for a single day and it would take eight days to go and fetch more oil. What was Judah to do?

Judah lit the lamp. Then, an amazing thing happened. It did not go out at the end of the day! God kept the lamp burning for eight more days until Judah returned with more oil.

Notes for Parents and Teachers

About Judaism
Judaism is one of the world's oldest religions, originating some 4,000 years ago in the Middle East. According to Jewish belief, God chose a man named Abraham, the leader of a nomadic people called the Hebrews, to be the father of the Jews. Jewish people believe in one God who created the world and cares for it. They believe that God made a covenant (agreement) with Abraham that the Jews would be his chosen people if they loved God and led holy lives. The Jews believe that they were chosen by God to set an example of holiness in the world. Anyone born of a Jewish mother is Jewish according to Jewish law, even if they do not actively practice their religion. Conversion to Judaism is possible.

About the stories in this book
In each of the world's religions, stories play an essential part. For centuries, they have been used to teach people about the traditions and beliefs of their religion in an accessible way, making difficult ideas and concepts easier to understand. For children in today's multicultural society, these stories also provide an ideal introduction to different religions' traditions, beliefs, and key figures.

The Story of Joseph
The story of Joseph is found in the Torah (Genesis 37–45). The Torah comprises the first five books of the Tenakh (Hebrew Bible) and is the most important part of Jewish scripture. The Torah contains stories from Jewish history and laws for Jews to live by. Joseph's story deals with several themes, including the importance of being genuinely sorry for doing wrong. Joseph tests his brothers to see if they have learned their lesson. When he sees that they are truly sorry, he forgives them for their treatment of him.

The Baby in the Basket
The story of the birth and life of Moses is found in the Torah, in the book of Exodus. The full story tells of the Jews' escape from slavery in Egypt, under Moses' leadership. It explores themes of leadership and obedience. Moses, who received the Ten Commandments from God, became one of the Jews' greatest leaders. Initially, Moses was reluctant to take on the role God gave him of leading the Jews out of Egypt. He felt that he was not worthy, but God gave him strength and guidance.

The Story of Esther
This tale is told in the Tenakh, in the Book of Esther. The story shows God using Esther to save the Jewish people from persecution. It is read in the synagogue at the festival of Purim, which falls in February or March. This is a joyful time when Jews celebrate the triumph of good over evil. Every time the name of Haman is read, children are encouraged to drown out his name with booing and by shaking rattles. Special foods eaten at Purim include triangular pastries stuffed with honey and fruit. These are called Hamantaschen (Haman's pockets).

The Temple Lamp
The story of the Temple lamp appears in the Talmud, a collection of writings about Jewish laws, ethics, customs, and history. The story deals with the theme of people standing up for what they believe in, even when their lives are under threat because of their beliefs. Despite persecution, the Jews refuse to give up their faith. The story is remembered at the winter festival of Hanukkah. Jews celebrate the miracle of the oil as the triumph of Jewish spiritual values in the face of attempts to destroy them. They light candles on a special candlestick, called a menorah, during the eight days of the festival.

Further things to do
• Read the stories to the children and then talk about them. Ask the children questions about what they think the stories mean. For example, what made Moses such a good leader?
• Relate the stories to experiences in the children's own lives. For example, have they ever done something wrong, then been sorry for it? Or, have they stuck up for a friend or something they liked, even though they were teased for it?
• Use a variety of methods to tell the stories. The children could act out the stories, making masks and costumes for their characters to wear. The story of Esther is acted out at Purim, with dress-up parties and plays.
• Decorate the classroom or home for Hanukkah. The children could make their own menorah out of cardboard and decorate them. They could also learn to play dreidel, a game traditionally played at Hanukkah, and find out about special Hanukkah foods. Extend this activity to investigate other Jewish festivals, especially the three "Pilgrim Festivals" (Sukkot, Pesach, and Shavuot), which are associated with the Exodus from Egypt.